NnOoPp
QqRr
SsTtUu
VvWw
XxYyZz

volume **7**

BIG BIRD'S SESAME STREET DICTIONARY

FEATURING JIM HENSON'S SESAME STREET MUPPETS

LETTERS R–S

by **Linda Hayward**

illustrated by **Joe Mathieu**

Editor in Chief: Sharon Lerner

Art Directors: Grace Clarke and Cathy Goldsmith
with special thanks to Judith M. Leary

Funk & Wagnalls, Inc./Children's Television Workshop

Rr

A B C D E F G H I J K L M N O P Q **R** S T U V W X Y Z

rabbit   A rabbit is a furry animal with long ears.

race   A race is a contest to see who is the fastest.

The **rabbits** are about to have a **race**.

radio   A radio is a machine. When you turn on a radio, you can hear music or voices.

Bert is listening to the Pigeon News on the **radio**.

railroad   A railroad is a track for trains. A track is made with long metal strips called rails.

Look up the word train.

The **railroad** workers are working on the **railroad**.

rain   Rain is water that falls in drops from clouds.

rainbow   A rainbow is a strip of colors that you sometimes see in the sky when it rains.

raincoat   A raincoat is a coat that keeps you from getting wet when it rains.

rake   A rake is a tool used to make the ground smooth or clear.

Big Bird is using a **rake** to **rake** away the leaves.

ranch   A ranch is a place for raising animals.

Rodeo Rosie lives on a **ranch**.

raw   Food that is raw is not cooked.

Rodeo Rosie gives her horse **raw** carrots to eat.

8 reach

reach When you reach, you stretch out a part of your body to take or touch something.

Cookie Monster can **reach** the cookie jar on the top shelf.

When are we going to **reach** the next restaurant?

Reach also means to arrive at a place.

FOOD FUEL 5 MI.

read When you read, you understand the words you see.

I I ... can can ... read read.

i can read

I can **read**!

ready If you are ready to do something, you have everything you need to do it.

Hey, Bert! Are you **ready** to go to the costume party?

I'm **ready.**

Bert is not a **real** pigeon.

Bernice is a **real** pigeon.

real Real means true. A real thing is not make-believe.

really Really means truly.

That's a **really** scary monster costume you are wearing.

This is not a costume. I **really** am a monster.

reason When you know why something happens, you know the reason.

Give me a **reason** why I should believe you are a real witch.

Oh!

recipe A recipe tells you how to make something to eat.

> Hey, Bert. What are you doing?

> I'm trying a new **recipe** for oatmeal ice cream.

COOKING WITH OATMEAL

record A record is a round, flat piece of plastic that can be played on a record player to make music.

> I love to listen to my **record** of Chris and the Alphabeats.

I was born to add...

rectangle A rectangle is a shape with four sides and four square corners.

> Three of these things belong together. One of these things is not the same.

Three of these shapes are **rectangles**.
A circle is not a **rectangle**.
The circle does not belong.

refrigerator A refrigerator is a machine that keeps food cold.

> Ernie, don't forget to close the door of the **refrigerator**.

MILK

relative Your relatives are the people in your family.

> These are pictures of some of my **relatives**.

UNCLE UNO   FATHER   MOTHER   COUSIN

remember When you remember, you think of something that happened in the past.

> I **remember** when my Uncle Uno gave me my first counting toy.

rent When you rent something, you pay to use it. You do not own it.

> When did you get the new bicycle, Betty Lou?

> It's not mine, Farley. I just **rented** it for today.

repair Repair means fix.

Prairie Dawn can **repair** a broken chair.

GLUE

rest When you rest, you nap or stay quiet for a while.

Big Bird needs to **rest** every afternoon.

rest The rest of something is everything that is left.

Hey, waiter! There is only one letter in my alphabet soup. Where is the **rest** of the alphabet?

Here are the **rest** of the letters, sir!

restaurant A restaurant is a place where you can buy and eat a meal.

Grover the waiter works in a **restaurant.**

return When you return, you come back after being away. When you return something, you give it back.

I wonder when Ernie will **return.**

Sorry I'm late, Bert. I had to **return** the hammer I borrowed from Biff.

rhinoceros   A rhinoceros is a big animal with thick skin and one or two horns on the top of its nose.

rhyme   Words that rhyme sound alike at the end.

*I have been trying to think of a word that **rhymes** with **rhinoceros,** but it's imposserous—*

I mean, impossible.

Hat!

*...**rhymes** with bat!*

Duckie!

*...**rhymes** with yucchy!*

ribbon   A ribbon is a narrow piece of cloth or paper.

Bert tied a **ribbon** around his present for Ernie.

rice   Rice is a kind of grain. Rice grows above the ground in shallow water. Some cereals are made from rice.

Betty Lou is picking **rice.**

rich   When you are rich, you have lots of money.

*If I were **rich,** I would buy the biggest box of oatmeal in the whole world.*

Gourmet OATMEAL
.IMPORTED.
"FOR THE DISCRIMINATING PALATE"
JUMBO SIZE!

riddle   A riddle is a question that is also a puzzle.

ride   When you ride, you sit or stand while something carries you along.

Here's a monster **riddle.**

How can four big monsters **ride** in one tiny car?

Two in front and two in back!

right   When something is right, it is correct. It is not wrong.

Grover, you had two big boxes, and I gave you two more. Now you have four big boxes. **Right?**

That's **right!**

right   Right is also a direction. It is the opposite of left.

This is my **right** hand.

This is my **right** foot.

Right away means at once or immediately.

ring   A ring is a circle.

Rodeo Rosie is in the center of the **ring.**

Ring around a Rosie ...

A **ring** that you wear is a circle that fits around your finger.

ring   When something rings, it makes the sound of a bell.

Three of these things belong together. One of these things is not the same.

A telephone, a cowbell, and a bicycle bell are things that **ring.** A banana does not **ring.** The banana does not belong.

river   A river is a large stream of water that flows into another river, a lake, or an ocean.

Prairie Dawn is paddling her canoe up the **river.**

road   A road is a man-made path between two places.
It is wide enough for automobiles and trucks to ride on.

The Count is driving his bat car along the **road.**

robot   A robot is a machine that can
follow orders to do certain kinds of work.

Sam the **robot** can
do many things
that people can do.

rock   A rock is a piece of stone. A rock is
hard and comes out of the ground.

rock   When you rock, you move back and
forth or from side to side.

Farley likes to **rock**
in a **rocking** chair.

rocket   A rocket is a machine that moves through the air or up into space. Sometimes rockets go to the moon or other planets.

The **rocket** is taking off.

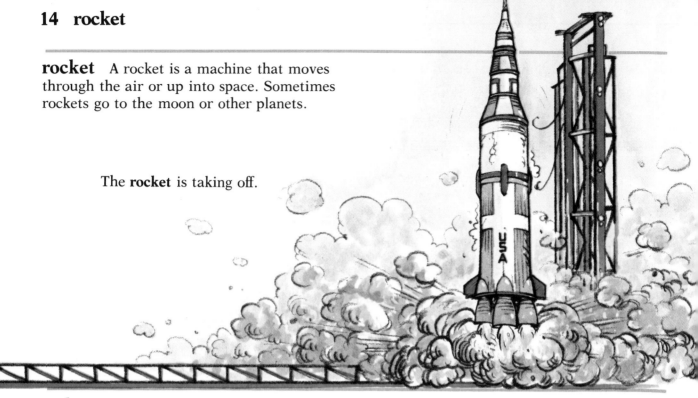

rodeo   A rodeo is a show in which cowgirls and cowboys ride horses and rope steers.

Come and see the **rodeo**!

roll   When something rolls, it turns over and over as it moves along.

Betty Lou's ball started to **roll** down the hill, and Barkley chased it.

roof   A roof is the top covering for a building.

Biff is fixing the **roof.**

room A room is space inside a building. A room is surrounded by walls.

This **room** belongs to my cat, Fatatatita.

root A root is the part of a plant that is under the ground. Plants take in food through their roots. Some roots can be eaten.

rope A rope is a strong, thick cord that can be used to tie things together.

Herry Monster forgot to untie the **rope.**

rough Rough means not smooth.

This ground is very **rough** and bumpy.

round Something round is shaped like a ball or a circle.

Three of these things belong together. One of these things is not the same.

An orange, a ring, and a wheel are **round.**
A book is not **round.**
The book does not belong.

row A row is a line of people or things.

There is a **row** of birds on Bert's clothesline.

row When you row, you move a boat by pulling oars through the water.

Herry likes to **row** his **row**boat.

rubber Rubber is something that stretches and is waterproof. Many things are made out of rubber.

Rubber boots.

Rubber ball.

Rubber band.

Rubber Duckie.

rug A rug is a cover for the floor. A rug can cover the whole floor or a part of it.

Bert likes to vacuum the **rug.**

ruler A ruler is a tool with straight edges. It is used for measuring length. Look up the word length.

This board is two feet long.

The carpenter is using a **ruler.** She is measuring the length of a board.

run When you run, you move very quickly on your feet.

Marshal Grover can **run** fast. Fred can **run** faster.

Whoa, Fred! Wait for me!

This is ridiculous! How can you have a dictionary without words like rude and rubbish and rotten? I am going to read something *really* interesting.

THE ROTTEN EGG AND I

AH-CHOO!

A B C D E F G H I J K L M N O P Q R **S** T U V W X Y Z

sad   When you are sad, you feel unhappy.

Big Bird is **sad.**
He did not
get a letter from
Snuffle-upagus.

SNIFF

BIG BIRD

safe   Safe means not in danger.

The little pig is **safe.**
The big bad wolf cannot
blow his house down.

sail   A sail is a piece of cloth
that catches the wind.

sailboat   A sailboat is a boat
with one or more sails.

Prairie Dawn's
sailboat has
one **sail.**

P.D.

salt   Salt is tiny white grains that come
from the ground or from sea water. Some
people put salt on food because they like
the way it tastes.

Sully is shaking **salt**
on his hard-boiled egg.

same   When things are the same, they are like each other.

Cookie and Grover are wearing the **same** tie.

sand   Sand is made of tiny grains of rock. You can find sand in the desert or at the beach.

Betty Lou likes to play in the **sand** at the beach.

sandwich   A sandwich is two pieces of bread with some other food in between.

Here is my favorite **sandwich**—sardines and sour pickles on stinkweed bread!

save   When you save something, you keep it in a safe place.

Bert **saves** bricks.

save   Save also means to rescue someone or something from danger.

Uh-oh! There is someone who needs my help. I will **save** her.

HELP! HELP! Somebody **save** me from this furry blue monster!

saw   A saw is a tool. It is made of metal and has teeth for cutting.

Prairie Dawn is cutting a board with a **saw**.

say Say means speak.

scale A scale is a machine that is used to weigh people or things.

Snuffle-upagus is standing on a **scale.** How much does he weigh?

scare Something that scares you is something that makes you afraid.

school A school is a place where you go to learn things from teachers.

scissors Scissors are a tool used for cutting. Scissors have two handles and two blades.

scream When you scream, you make a loud noise with your voice.

sea   A sea is a very large body of salt water.

I like to swim in the **sea.**

Sea and ocean are two names for the same thing.

season   A season is a time of the year.
There are four seasons: winter, spring, summer, and fall.

Farmer Grover works hard every **season.**

WINTER   SPRING   SUMMER   FALL

seat   A seat is something to sit on.

Three of these things belong together. One of these things is not the same.

The stool, the chair, and the bench are all kinds of **seats.** A cactus is not a good thing to sit on. The cactus does not belong.

second A second is a very small amount of time. There are sixty seconds in a minute.

The Count is counting the **seconds** on his bat clock.

One, two, three, four, five, six ...

tick tock

second Second also means the one that comes right after the first.

Betty Lou is first in line. Barkley is **second.**

ICE CREAM

secret A secret is a special thing you know but do not tell.

I have a special hiding place, but you do not know where it is. It is my **secret.**

see When you look at something, you see it.

Whoops! Now you can **see** my **secret** hiding place. It is not a **secret** anymore.

seed A seed is the special part of a plant that can grow into a new plant.

Farmer Grover plants **seeds** in the spring.

selfish If you are selfish, you care about yourself and not about other people.

Cookie Monster! Don't be **selfish**! The cookies are for everyone.

COOKIES

sell When you sell something, you give it to someone and that person gives you money for it. After you sell something, it does not belong to you anymore.

I have to **sell** some of my old trash to make room for my new trash.

GARBAGE SALE

send   When you send something, you start it on its way.

I will **send** a thank-you note to Granny Bird because she **sent** me some birdseed cookies.

set   A set is a group of things that are alike in some way.

I have a **set** of blue dishes.

I have a **set** of yellow dishes.

seven   Seven is a number. Seven is one more than six.

seventeen   Seventeen is a number. Seventeen is ten plus seven more.

Bert has ten red bricks and **seven** gray bricks. He has **seventeen** bricks all together.

7
GRAY
BRICKS
↓

10
RED
BRICKS
↓

17
BRICKS

sew   When you sew, you use a needle to pull thread through cloth or other material. You can sew by hand or by machine.

The Amazing Mumford has to **sew** a new button on his cape.

shadow   A shadow is a dark shape. When a light shines on something, it makes a shadow on the other side.

Egad! Look at that **shadow** on the wall. I think someone is following me.

shake   When you shake something, you move it quickly back and forth or up and down.

Ernie has to **shake** the dust out of the mop.

cough!

shape   The form of something is its shape.

Here are some of my favorite **shapes**.

CIRCLE   SQUARE

RECTANGLE

DIAMOND   STAR

share   When you share something, you let others use it or have part of it.

Here, Sully. I will **share** my sandwich with you if you will **share** that apple with me.

shallow   Something that is shallow is not deep.

The water in this wading pool is too **shallow** for swimming.

Not if you are a little bird.

sharp   Something that is sharp has a thin cutting edge or a point on the end.

Hey, you! Wanna buy this knife? It's so **sharp,** it will cut, peel, slice, chop, saw....

I don't want to buy a knife. But how much is all that wonderful garbage??

she   She is another way to say woman or girl or female animal.

Prairie Dawn is busy. **She** is making a home for her pet spider.

sheep   A sheep is an animal that has four legs and is covered with wool.

I am a baby **sheep**. I am a lamb.

I am the lamb's mother. I am a ewe.

I am the lamb's father. I am a ram.

shell   A shell is a hard covering. Some animals have shells. Some eggs have shells. Some seeds have shells.

Oscar, look at my collection of sea**shells**.

I have a **shell** collection, too, Betty Lou— egg**shells**!

shine   When something shines, it makes a bright light. Something can also shine if light bounces off it.

Marshal Grover's badge **shines** because it is so clean.

ship   A ship is a large boat. Some ships have sails and some have engines. Some have both.

Captain Bert's **ship** is sailing into the harbor.

shirt   A shirt is a piece of clothing you wear on the top part of your body.

shoe   A shoe is something you wear on your foot.

Ernie is wearing a striped **shirt** and one saddle **shoe.**

shop   A shop is a store where you can buy things.

Cookie Monster loves to go **shopping** at the cookie **shop.**

short   Something that is short is not as high as something that is tall.

When something is short, the beginning is close to the end.

Big Bird is tall. Little Bird is **short.** Little Bird's jump rope is too **short** for Big Bird.

shoulder   Your shoulder is a part of your body. Your arms are attached to your shoulders. Look up the word body.

The Count's pet bat is sitting on his **shoulder.**

shout   When you shout, you call out loudly.

MUD! FRESH MUD! GET YOUR MUD HERE!

I love to hear the Mudman **shout.**

FRESH MUD

shovel   A shovel is a tool used to scoop things up.

Farmer Grover is using his snow **shovel** to **shovel** snow.

show   When you show something, you put it where it can be seen.

Let me **show** you my seashell collection.

Let me **show** you my nutshell collection.

show   A show is something special to be seen or heard. A show can be a movie, a play, or a program on radio or television.

Grover Knover is putting on a **show.** Everyone is watching.

HURRAY!

shut   When you shut something, you close it.

I must **shut** the barn door so the cows will not get out.

sick   When you are sick, you are not healthy.

Biff is **sick.** He has a cold.

Get Well Soon Sully

side   The side of something is the part that is not the top, bottom, front, or back.

Herry Monster is lifting a chest. There are two handles— one on each **side.**

Side can also mean the team you are on.

Hurray for our **side!**

sign   A sign tells you something. A printed sign uses words or pictures. You can also make signs with your hands in special ways.

What do these **signs** tell you?

STOP

When you **sign** your name, you write your name.

silent   Silent means without any sound.

Shhhhh! We must be **silent** while Mr. Snuffle-upagus takes his nap!

silly   When something is silly, it does not make sense and may be funny.

Fred, what happened to your head?

Isn't Marshal Grover **silly**?

sing   When you sing, you make music with your voice.

Bert likes to **sing** to Bernice. Bernice thinks he is a good **singer**.

Doin' the Pigeon ...

single   Single is a word that means one.

I would like a **single** scoop of birdseed ice cream, please.

sink   A sink is a bowl that can be filled with water and has a drain to let the water out.

Cookie the baker has a **sink** full of dirty dishes.

sink   When something sinks, it goes down. In water, some things float and some things sink.

Grover's rowboat is beginning to **sink**.

sister   If your mother and father have another child who is a girl, she is your sister.

She is my **sister**.

He is my brother.

sit When you sit, you rest on the lower part of your body. Your weight is off your feet.

Why did the monster **sit** on the clock?

He wanted to be on time!

crunch!

six Six is a number. Six is one more than five.

sixteen Sixteen is a number. Sixteen is ten plus six more.

Oscar has ten red apple cores and **six** green apple cores. He has **sixteen** apple cores all together.

size The size of something is how big or how small it is.

Figgy Fizz comes in three different **sizes**— small, medium, and large.

skate A skate is something you wear on your foot to help you move on ice, hard floors, or sidewalks. Some skates have runners and some have wheels.

Betty Lou wears roller **skates** to **skate** on the sidewalk.

Farley wears ice **skates** to **skate** on the ice.

skeleton Your skeleton is all the bones of your body fitted together. All people and most animals have skeletons. Look up the word bone.

This is a picture of a human **skeleton**.

This is a picture of a dinosaur **skeleton**.

skin Your skin is the outer covering of your body. Animals and fruits and vegetables also have skins.

My pet snake, Sammy, has pretty stripes on his **skin**.

I do not have stripes on my **skin**.

skip   When you skip, you take little hops while you run.

I like to walk.

I like to **skip**.

When you **skip** something, you leave it out.

I read the whole dictionary and didn't **skip** one word.

skirt   A skirt is a piece of clothing. It hangs from your waist.

Rodeo Rosie is wearing a brown **skirt.**

sled   A sled is something with runners that slides on the snow or the ice.

Betty Lou is coasting down the hill on her **sled.**

sky   The sky is the covering of air and clouds over the world.

I love to fly my little airplane in the **sky.**

sleep   When you sleep, you close your eyes and rest your whole body.

Grover likes to **sleep** with his teddy bear.

slide   Slide means to move smoothly across a surface.

slide   A slide is a playground toy. After you climb to the top, you slide to the bottom.

Big Bird likes to **slide** down the **slide.**

slip   When you slip, you slide and start to fall.

slippery   Something that is slippery can make you slip.

OOOPS!

Banana peels are **slippery.** If you step on one, you may **slip.**

slow   Slow means not fast.

Barkley is watching a snail race. Snails are **slow.**

woof!

1   2   3   4

small Small means little.

Big Bird has a large mailbox.

Little Bird has a **small** mailbox.

smell When you smell something, you breathe an odor in through your nose.

Can you **smell** my stinkweek soup? Doesn't it have a lovely **smell**?

PHEW!

smile When you smile, the corners of your mouth turn up and you look happy.

Rubber Duckie makes Ernie **smile**.

smoke Smoke is the cloud that rises from something burning.

Prairie Dawn's campfire is still burning. She can see the **smoke**.

Where there's **smoke,** there's fire.

smooth Something that is smooth has a surface that is not rough or wrinkled or bumpy.

The sidewalk is **smooth**.

The road is bumpy.

sneeze When you sneeze, air comes out of your nose and mouth and you make a loud sound like AH-CHOO.

Pepper makes you ... ah ... AH ... AH ... CHOOOO! ... **sneeze**.

snow Snow is tiny white flakes of frozen water that fall from the clouds.

so So means very.

> I love the **snow—so, so** much.

soap Soap is something used with water to clean things.

Ernie is cleaning Rubber Duckie with **soap.**

sock A sock is something made of cloth that you wear on your foot. You put on your sock before you put on your shoe.

There is a hole in the Count's **sock.**

> 1 ... one hole! Wonderful!

soft When something is soft, it is not hard or stiff.

Three of these things belong together. One of these things is not the same.

A teddy bear, a pillow, and a blanket are all **soft** things. A lunchbox is a hard thing. The lunchbox does not belong.

son If a father and mother have a child who is a boy, that child is their son.

> They are my parents.

> He is our **son.**

song A song is something to sing.

soon Soon is a word that means not too long from now.

> Doin' the Pigeon ... doin' the Pigeon ...

> When will this **song** be over?

> Soon.

sorry When you are sorry, you are sad about something that has happened.

I'm **sorry** I broke your toy airplane, Farley. I'll try to fix it.

sound A sound is something you hear.

Hey, Oscar! What was that terrible **sound** I heard a moment ago?

I didn't hear anything, Betty Lou. I was too busy playing my trombone.

soup Soup is a liquid food made by cooking meat, vegetables, or fruits in water.

Hey, waiter! There's a fly in my **soup.**

Don't worry, sir. Flies don't eat much.

speak When you speak, you talk.

I will now **speak** about my favorite subject— pigeons.

Happiness is...

In the beginning...

PIGEON *Lovers'* CLUB

special Special is a word that means not like all the others.

Mr. Snuffle-upagus is my **special** friend.

speed The speed of something is how fast it goes.

Grover Knover can move with great **speed.**

spell When you spell a word, you say or write its letters in the right order.

Oscar can **spell** SCRAM.

S-C-R-A-M! SCRAM!

spider A spider is a very small animal with eight legs. Many spiders spin webs to catch insects for food.

I am Miss Muffet. This is my pet **spider,** Stanley.

The SESAME STREET PLAYERS in Little Miss Muffet

spill When something spills, it falls out of a container—usually by mistake.

Farley did not want to **spill** his jellybeans. But he did.

spin When you spin something, you turn it around and around quickly.
When something spins, it turns around quickly.

Ernie likes to **spin** his top. His top is **spinning** fast.

spoon A spoon is a tool used to stir or scoop up food. You sometimes use a spoon when you eat.

Bert eats his oatmeal with a **spoon.**

spot A spot is a kind of mark.

Look! There is a **spot** on my cape. Let me count it. 1...one **spot**! Wonderful!

spread When you spread something, you smooth it out so that it covers more space.

Bert likes to **spread** peanut butter on a piece of bread.

PEANUT BUTTER

spring   Spring is the name of a season. Spring comes after winter.

The leaves on the trees are beginning to grow. It must be **spring.**

square   A square is a shape with four corners and four sides of the same length.

One of these shapes is not like the others. One of these shapes does not belong.

The circle does not have four corners and four sides. It is not a **square.** It does not belong.

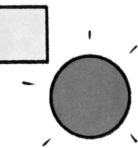

squeeze   When you squeeze something, you press it.

Ernie has to **squeeze** the sponge to get the water out.

stage   A stage is the place in the theater where the actors act, the dancers dance, and the singers sing.

To fly or not to fly …

Big Bird is acting on the **stage.**

stairs   Stairs are a set of steps. You can go up stairs and you can go down stairs.

These are the **stairs** to the castle tower. Let me count the steps. 1 … one step … 2 … two steps …

stamp   A stamp is a small piece of paper that you put on a letter or package to show that you have paid to send it.

stand   When you stand, you are on your feet, but your feet are not moving.

Farley has to **stand** in line to buy a **stamp** for his letter.

stamp

star A star is another sun—far, far away. At night a star looks like a tiny point of light in the sky.

Grover the astronaut can see many **stars.**

star A star is also a shape.

Grover's spaceship has a **star** on its side.

A **star** is also a famous person in a show.

clap clap clap
HURRAY!
clap YEA!

start When you start something, you begin it or get it going.

Grouches, **start** your grouchmobiles so I can **start** the race.

STARTER

START

stay When you stay, you do not leave.

Connie the witch is going on a trip. The other witches will **stay** at home.

steal When someone steals, that person takes something that does not belong to him or her.

Watch out for the Cookie Thief! He might **steal** your cookies.

COOKIES

WANTED
The Great
COOKIE
THIEF

step A step is what you put your foot on when you go up or down stairs.

The stairs in my castle have five hundred and sixty-eight **steps.** I love to count them all. 1 ... one **step** ... 2 ...two **steps** ...

stick   A stick is a long, thin piece of wood.

Barkley likes to play with a **stick.**

stick   When you make something stick, it stays where you put it.

How do you like my latest work of art? I used glue to make all these pieces of garbage **stick** to my hat.

still   Still means not moving or not talking.

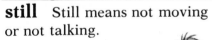

Hold **still,** everybody!

stone   A stone is a rock. Some things are made out of stone.

Farmer Grover is lifting a heavy **stone.**

stop   When something stops, it does not keep going.

Grover Knover has to **stop** at the **stop** sign.

store   A store is a place where you can buy things.

Grover's mother bought a new book at the book**store.**

story A story is something to tell. Stories can be true or imaginary. You can tell a story out loud or write it.

stove A stove is a thing used for cooking or heating.

Grover's mother is reading the **story** of Goldilocks and the three bears.

Papa Bear was cooking porridge on the **stove.**

straight Straight means without a bend or a curve or a curl or a twist.

This is a **straight** line. The other lines are not **straight.**

straight line

crooked line
curly line
curved line

strange Strange means odd, unusual, or not seen or heard before.

There is a **strange** bird in Big Bird's nest.

A **stranger** is someone you don't know.

Hi. My name is Fred.

BUS STOP

street A street is a road in a town or a city. A street usually has buildings on it.

Sesame **Street** is a nice **street** to live on.

HOOPER'S STORE

SESAME STREET

123

stretch When you stretch something, you make it longer or bigger.

Don't put my sweater on, Herry. You will **stretch** it.

string   A string is a very thin rope.

Big Bird is tying a package with **string**.

strong   Strong means having lots of power or not easily broken.

Herry can lift heavy barbells.
Herry is **strong**.

The third little pig's house was **strong**. The wolf could not blow it down.

subtract   When you subtract, you take something away.

If I **subtract** one apple from four apples, I will have three apples.

$$\begin{array}{r} 4 \\ -1 \\ \hline 3 \end{array}$$

subway   A subway is an underground railroad. Some cities have subways.

Biff rides to work on the **subway**.

suddenly   Suddenly means all at once.

The Monster Marching Band had to stop **suddenly**.

CRASH!

sugar Sugar is something you can put in food to make it taste sweeter.

summer Summer is the name of a season. Summer comes after spring.

sun The sun is a star. It gives light and warmth and energy to all living things on the earth.

The **sun** is the brightest light in the sky.

super Super means extra-big, extra-strong, extra-smart, or extra-good.

sure When you are sure about something, you know that it is true. You are certain.

surprise A surprise is something you do not know about or expect.

swallow When you swallow food or water, it goes down your throat to your stomach.

Sammy the snake will now **swallow** another apple.

sweep To sweep means to brush away. You can use a broom to sweep dirt.

This is the way I **sweep** my nest, **sweep** my nest, **sweep** my nest....

swim When you swim, you use your arms and legs to move through the water.

Prairie Dawn likes to **swim.** She is a good **swimmer.**

swing A swing is a hanging seat that moves back and forth.

What time is it when Herry Monster sits on your **swing**?

Time to get a new **swing.**

sweet When something is sweet, it is nice to taste or smell or hear or see. When something tastes sweet, it usually has sugar in it.

How **sweet!**

sniff!

How **sweet!**

Tweet Tweet Tweet

How **sweet!**

How **sweet!**

Just think of all the super words that begin with S— scummy, slimy, sloppy, soggy, stinky, swampy— and my special favorite— SCRAM!

Ernie and Bert at the Seashore

How many things that begin with the letters **R** or **S** can you find in this picture?